In the Scaffolding

Also by Eric Miller

Song of the Vulgar Starling

In the Scaffolding

ERIC MILLER

Copyright © Eric Miller, 2005.

All rights reserved. No part of this work may be reproduced or used in any form or by any means, electronic or mechanical, including photocopying, recording, or any retrieval system, without the prior written permission of the publisher or a licence from the Canadian Copyright Licensing Agency (Access Copyright). To contact Access Copyright, visit www.accesscopyright.ca or call 1-800-893-5777.

Edited by Ross Leckie.
Cover illustration, *Land of Nod* (detail) by François Thisdale, 2004.
Cover design by Julie Scriver.
Book design by Lisa Rousseau.
Printed in Canada by AGMV Marquis.
10 9 8 7 6 5 4 3 2 1

Library and Archives Canada Cataloguing in Publication

Miller, Eric, 1961-
In the scaffolding / Eric Miller.

Poems.
ISBN 0-86492-425-9

I. Title.

PS8576.I5372I6 2005   C811'.54   C2005-900693-5

Published with the financial support of the Canada Council for the Arts, the Government of Canada through the Book Publishing Industry Development Program, and the New Brunswick Culture and Sports Secretariat.

Goose Lane Editions
469 King Street
Fredericton, New Brunswick
CANADA E3B 1E5

www.gooselane.com

In memory of my father

Contents

Spring's Compartments of Music

- 13 Late in the Season Yet Another Defence of Nature Writing
- 14 The Question
- 15 In the Scaffolding
- 17 Ducks
- 18 The Web
- 19 The Stinger
- 20 Voices
- 21 Swan Speech
- 23 The Woodlot, Fredericton
- 25 Cryptogamia
- 28 Theodicy in New Brunswick
- 30 Celestial Navigators
- 32 March Forest
- 34 Winter Wren and Spring Rain
- 36 Rain after Clear
- 37 History of Petals
- 38 Jupiter the Woodpecker
- 39 Bushtits
- 41 Lagoon

The Broken Eggs of the World

- 45 Sleep Sink
- 46 Sunday Afternoon
- 48 Colborne Street
- 50 The Tongue
- 51 The Bluffs
- 52 The Beaverpond
- 54 The Outcrop

First and Last Things

- 59 Night Park
- 61 Cara
- 63 Deliverance
- 64 Holotype
- 66 Hortus Botanicus
- 69 Gorgias the Magician
- 71 Styx
- 73 No Memory of Pleasure Imprisons
- 75 Wrong
- 77 Hunted
- 78 Thaw

Infancy's Visionary Tactility

- 83 A Baby's Bent Head
- 84 Rock, Ball
- 86 Reading
- 87 September in Uplands Park
- 88 Wading Willows Beach
- 90 Primaries
- 91 Pointer

- 93 Acknowledgements

In the Scaffolding

Spring's Compartments of Music

Late in the Season Yet Another Defence of Nature Writing

Where are the songs of spring? Not over
nor is it good to pronounce "They're
over." They are, they are
here in October. And as the berry
swells after the rotten flower, hairy and sticky
the berry and stained and seeping ranker
perfume and a preferable one to the funereal expansions
of spring, so is the whisper song — the casual
fallen-apart flock song, the placeless
song loosed from the stations of its nesting
insistence among the weightlessly
tailspinning leaves and the webs
gumming impalpability to the frond's broken stave —

so is the lost-cause song to the definite
territories, spring's compartments of music.

Let there be no elegy for what is not dead but freed, for
elegy is a danger and it spreads like a smell and enters every nostril
even as song fills a forest and it becomes a berry in whose drink we all
ferment.

October song tingles on the ear like tartness and snapped webs
and you, you think an elegy needful.
But the elegy is killing us, dead audience.

These dead will outlive that mortal unseasonable song of yours
even as you lower yourself into a casket like a dead nest
to be buried among the countable but forever unnumbered berries
that lapse into mould from their shapes and stink well and poorly of eternal life.

The Question

The angel, what I thought was an angel, hovered
over me and asked, For you what happiness?
And I heard its cries of a gull in whose sky-blank
span we lie, a bird the colour of driftwood
among peeled, bleached driftwood clouds and the foam
the waves edge up onto outcrop rock at the point
of land, foam gull-feather-coloured and carrying
fallen feathers and silent the other birds
in close to me among the salt-burned spirea,
those near birds being sparrows, a song sparrow
and a tree sparrow. I saw the dark seed
focus in the sparrows' heads and slight they moved
into and out of mean limbs of the rattled
bush saying nothing. The wind thumbed them
as if sorting the feathers of their napes and flanks.
The cries of the gull glittered and slid hard
like mica then soft as pressed skin and was the gull
angel? I said, Happy now in the boat
that has capsized in the surf the angels permeate
with their song. The waves danced the dance
of close and far and the sparrows hopped in the wind
as securely on the rock as a fly that walks the floor now a ceiling.
The bush shook in the condescension of primeval
courtesy, though its necessity was rooted spindlier
than wind and gull's music, which changed as the sparrows
changed, into my answer, the vibrating, sparkling, drab-in-glory
that was the angel's beak-blown question.

In the Scaffolding

> "It was very difficult for Wallace to give his full sense of that garden into which he came." — H.G. Wells, "The Door in the Wall"

As when you come to an autumn boathouse and ice
has begun to suppress the inventiveness of water
but, crammed in the crannies, the hard shells
and soft shapes of swallow nests deck the cold beams,
belvederes of instinct's cyclical Babylon,
stuck even in winter with summer's bright cockade,
borrowed and forfeited breast-, wing- and tail-feathers,
and the stilled guano, expressive in collapse
as melted candle wax, moulds a lasting
testament to the outgoing febrility
of nestlings and the whole swallow-city rests
intact, ruinous only by the absence of birds
and the clement scaffold of their supporting season —

the estate of what has vanished and what remains
entrusted to you like a museum shelf of vases
the stout or slender evacuation of whose chambers
you can, with effort, replenish without pain,
from your own swallow-thronged experience —

so, as you step along this short road,
you pass from *plein-air* vessel to vessel of tree-odour,
each perfume dispersed and held in one gesture of fidelity,
embrace, release and retraction,
here the locus classicus of the poplar, that rooted acridity
bending in memory forever over the fathomless waist-deep of canal
marmoreally yet provisionally
inscribed with the breeze's latest last words
hardly rocking the duckweed,
and here the cedar, exuding from its green scales
the proportions of the hortus conclusus you want, always, to pace . . .

An immured garden opens, a recess only of scent,
walled with clear walls steep in evocation
where odour is a kind of stained glass, a partitioning lens,
under clouds that fume their own rooms of brilliant opacity
and among the birds whose songs expand a kingdom
founded in sound and lost in silence
and founded again in the mind that can recite them to itself
not quite at will
when snow closes smell into trees and swells its blockade
before boathouse doors.

Ducks

We love to service attractive greed.

The duck's back is not shaken,
not blurred by the avidity of its bill,
so even the crass keeps elegant in part,
and to gratify a creature as we would be gratified
satisfies another greed, a distillate of insatiability,
the nurse's hurt need of the patient,
breast's congested thirst for an infant,
until the greasy brown bag is crumpled, empty,
and the boy, no longer a magnet, a fountain of bread,
must impersonate his own duck, arms
behind back, feet splayed, quacking, laughing,
and those hungry gems seek appeasement elsewhere
in the sparkling eutrophic dump of the waters
where appetite gobbles oblivious to its own beauty
and shamelessness has nothing to be ashamed of
and to give is to receive, and bread cast on the waters
returns reflexively in the prismatic
theophany of webbed ruthlessness.

The Web

September's a month spun by spiders.

When you aren't looking, it is drawn tight.

Your nerves are caught and like stretched time
they snap.

The feeling then is neither finger nor hair
but the trace trick of elastic crystal, a trap,
and when you try to tear that touch away
it stays because it seems to have vanished
and the free inhuman hand that wove it
seizes your heart in supernumerary fear
and you wear the glinting, gridded mask
of a month to fix flies, glue flight,
hang the fruit like the traitor's body
and never let that ripe suspense fall
nor let bad kisses stop brushing the skin.

So the furry envenomed clutch can reach
and hold fast, diaphanously, mid-air,
meshing the wind, then stitching
possessive sutures to the deed of phobia,

each string as bright, thin, involved
as love's gummed strands and unguent.

The Stinger

The wasp is suited to its time of climax,
of something tottering in the doddering angers
of its toxic body striped in sugars
and carrion of last appetite, like the undertakers of Black Death
who fucked the bodies they dumped, the dead brought out,
knowing they would die soon and partner them faithfully,
rotten among children and family already stiff as firewood.

The wasp whines the dying hour of vacation
scrambling into apertures, feeling out
the cupped, failed, cracked eggs of the second chance at nesting,
shaking with hunger for what neither sex nor food nor thought can fill:
the desire for a better life in meat, more charged with gustier mind
and more slipperily carnal and more shiningly winged,
not like this, not with wings like wax wafers
veined with fumbled eyelashes to tremble in fury,
Icaruses who can neither fall fully nor rise high

but lift a sting poisoning themselves until they can pierce another
and die of relief in hot discharge of their disillusionment and summer's.

Voices

Something in autumn releases the voices of starlings.
Voices fall as meditative-delirious as leaves
yet rise again, as though seconded always in their plunge
by attentive, protective breezes of loyalty
the way parents groom their youngest gently,
coaxing the comb painlessly through long fibres.

Something in autumn shines from the hair of the child
and from the vanes of the grass blades
and from the fallen pear, liquefying, crystalline,
wasp-attended, so that air, whether breathed by us
or free of us, is golden, patchy and golden, softened
light and softer shadow — hilarity that makes
a moving hand and foot insubstantial
yet memorial in the motions they make, as though
unmade as they made their motions, like sound,

like the voices of starlings polishing the heavy fruit
that bright decay disguises as weightless and bird-voiced light.

Swan Speech

The mute swan's contours, as clean as a water-
lily's, the water tinged with refrigeration of green.
The swan's contours appeal and they unnerve,
membranous foot too large, too blanched
beneath the swell that coolly reserves its judgement.
Like teeth from the gums of a drowned rat's jaws,
the bird's unmanicured nails jut from curled toes.
The throat balances an arc of farce and grace,
the slither of ropy velvet ossifying to the bill's
horny orange with a tumorous black bulb and the eye
not chill, really, but like something glimpsed
through the coddling oil in which it rests.

The waters pass no verdict.
All is upheld in clearest
suspension. Buoyed by a recent rain, the water rises
up the chain of lakes on the last of which, a pond,
like a *jolie-laide* lotus the swan floats unfreighted . . .

And this scene mirrors the baby's faculty of speech,
the way speech emerges from appealing lips
formerly unvexed by the lexical. Words brim,
welling toward sense drop by drop as the mask
of the water ripples and there it glides, huge mute swan
stippled in lymph denied by bird-unguents its absorption.
The bird makes no sound as it approaches the shore
but the limpid liquid lifts it as though toward the swollen
lips of the sky, buoyancy disconcertingly lighter
and lighter yet acceptable in its crescendo and about to
spill over, waggling such scandalous feet,

into the domain of the undeniable. This really happened.
The baby (diaper as white-yellow as that berg of plumage),
gazing down at the swan from the pond bank on legs
whose apparent stalwartness supplies no firm
foundation, made possible the congruity saying: *Swan*.

The Woodlot, Fredericton

1.

Stately and wildly, some light touches
on fallen needles and the rising ferns,
and it swirls there like a potion of nostalgia —
for the present, flower of pollen,
monument of dust, a lightshaft disguised
among pineshafts. It finds what is soft
in the stoniest substance of the hardest time.
It reclines on endurance, endurance relaxes
under its ease, the texture of moss, the colour of gold,
gold in the woodland eye, gold in the shadow
which rests like a fly in its seraphic breastplate.

In this light's accounting not a needle is lost.
The flame descends from heaven and does not consume.
So Nineveh might have stood, not reduced to cinders.
The index of the sun signs the outcrop: Promised Land.

Let home intensified to the point of homelessness
startle like a fledgling from a nesthole.
The slip of a feather hovers on borrowed light.
Take the census of chaos: it is inductive
and therefore utterly just, a fallen sparrow.
The detail of the everyday dilates an afterlife,
a resinous pyre exalts the last and first testament
of the instant's inaugural expiration.
Let blame, too, alight. It scratches on the bark;
injure little. The sun's sword turns every way
in the mean midst of this garden as slowly
as powder moulders in the trunk the woodpecker probes.

Grasp the hilt of the sword: it is as fragrant
as a cone, as soft as the tufts of a tail in shapely
withdrawal, as mild and vital as a single breath,
as gentle and extreme as a song the ear
just reaches — that vireo is summer's coda, the last clause.

2.

The ray finds the truth and the way
through the hachure of trees.
Clearly everything falls,
the vestments of decision, be they
silk, be they armour,
lapse to the forest floor
into the grave of full comprehension,
the phoenix of light
evoking the living earth
unemphatically golden, uncloyingly mossy,
straight from the sun that can burn out an eye,
that the eye sees by, that the eye
dare not directly regard.

Cryptogamia

1.

Fact and fantasy wed as inconspicuously
as moss, which is a cryptogam by classification,
meaning: occult are its rites of love compared
with those of more flagrant plants. Moss,
earliest mercy of earth, bedrock's benefaction,
mineral-bright yet as mild as the flesh of the thigh
that curls toward mounded felicity — moss
lays a bed thickening thoughtfully for
the performance of fantasy's union with fact,
making both true. True as in loyal,
true as correct — a fit that's true — tomb
built before death came to life
and the great stone rolled from that tomb.

This lining of a nest outside the nest
lets the unprecedented fledgling plummet without pain
giving me pause when I leave moss behind
going into places where no moss can grow:

what was that in my mind I can still call moss?
Hidden, it is hidden and soft around my mind
like the plumage that gentles the spars and tendons
of a bird's frangibility before it scatters posthumously
the marrowless semblance of the wreck of a nest.

2.

It irradiated us, that lovedamp aurora
of earth. Spongy refulgence, moss sprung
colour from toppled trunks whose greenness
reached munificence towards us, supporting us
as though we deserved it, whatever our lives
had been and done, our green eyes stronger now
than our legs. Were those things we stepped over
logs — or effigies of logs wholly grown
from moss? — ex-arboreal souls flat
on their backs, beaming,
dreaming the resilience of Elysium
six or so metres, that is to say, infinitely
far beneath the spruces' tusks
tossing invidious malformation to gore
the same invulnerable wind that had marked them.

3.

I know about moss but knowledge dozes
whenever I see it glowing, growing its gradualness
instantly all over the yellowish bones
of my all-at-once obsolete knowledge. The touch
it mollifies as simply as drinking the mouth,
as a belly's plushness impersonally
radiating from the world never harshly.
Where you least expect it, in a patent ruin
of thirsts and refusals, moss cultures
latitude for lethargy, summoning
the vegetable element from the animal eye,
graft of green and patience, accommodation;

here there is room, incubation at the undermost
inn. Absolutes fold their knees, compress
their pained eyelids and this pure feel
of compromise prostrates us, consumes
our limbs in its all-tolerant pyre — vital
pillow, tissue of contemplative euphoria,
eliding without elision the chinks between
fantasy and fact, as lustred as eyes of almost-sleep,
laid on the stone like the furred rinse of beginning,

burnishing, cushioning the world between intensities
with the broad yielding mind and the glimmer
of endurance tenuous, thick and copulative.

Theodicy in New Brunswick

I. Always the quality of mercy lies beyond us.

II. Somewhere I made mistakes but the light
pitches my shadow against my eye as softly
as cattail velvet might pacify a cheek.

    I can't get tired of this steep immense afternoon
through which my error climbs looking for a weight
with which to be oppressed, not finding it.

III. Blizzard should have screwed down penalty
from on high. But the sky stands tall, opaque,
feathered with levity,
exempt from any fall.

IV. No one throws rocks. Instead rocks pitch a reprieve
of shadows. Permeable eclipse among which
unseasonable insects ramble as clauses
from an elaborate writ of pardon.

V. So voluminously, luminously are we emancipated.
From obvious consequence the world forever liberates.

    Not wrath, but satiation
from an unknown dish.

VI. Make no mistake.
　　 The day of judgement is suspended.
　　 That spruce gallows hangs only the balmy air.
　　 Blunted sun has forfeited the blow of decision.
　　 Of course such mercy lacks mercy
　　 hearing neither my confession nor yours.
　　 Crime the day has never heard of:
　　 event succeeds event.

VII. And that's the punishment
　　 glistening and darkening with a raven's
　　 innocence, croaking not once
　　 about the Gate of the Law or who
　　 may stand before it. How high
　　 the bird flaps over that tolerant
　　 threshold, light in its span
　　 of grave pigment, Nemesis

　　 of nothing.

Celestial Navigators

Night falls. Migrant whitethroats ping upward
to meet it, piping softly to the accompaniment
of stars which, like singers more sincere
than talented, waver in their vocation
of holding a note, a place. They have
endurance but they falter all the way
so that even as night gains confidence
the sky still shakes like a trembling aspen.

Yes, the stars convulse like leaves.
They swarm, they should evoke a shudder,
yet they affect us tranquilly, reflectively,
so that we wonder, almost, if we could see
our thoughts mirrored in the shards of glint
in a world from which depth perception
has been cancelled. Intimacy enters
like breath into the chest. Perceptions
hang like constellations and now

whitethroats on hidden brown wing stream
past us, their voices as meteors no bigger
than a sidelong glance gliding in the great
close vacuum among Orion's on-and-off
convictions. Their vita enters one cold ear
and leaves the other. Who can tell a streetlamp
from Polaris, lulled in the intimate arms
of the fathomless, which we can't evade
any more than the baby crushed against the chest
who squirms, flesh of the flesh that crams it
into love's vast adherence. How far below,

on the abysmal tar, lane, traffic-pattern of the night,
our shoes slap like ecstatic hearts
alternately exalted and cast down, wings
almost, while heaven decks the upper sides of things
tingling with the stars' invisible sensation
of confiding radiance in their mobile roost,
shivering silver, a constant retraction of light toes.

March Forest

1.

Ignorance, the empty nest never filled and forever perfect —
ignorance is reminded of itself
by the song of a bird it does not recognize.
The dead leaves stir circularly across the earth like a resurrection
that still respects the right of the dead to remain dead
in the special antiquity of being present to the hour, yet very old.
It is a stirring, a lifting, a turning,
a hovering like the breath of wind
in the plumage of a dead bird, the robin
that fat with song died in the claws of a hawk
and was cast to the ground, careless.
But the living birds move among disparate branches
like variously applicable fruit.

As confidentially as spider floss on skin
the sun discloses the chambers it tints.
Sparsities, grandeurs.
The sense of sparse, of grand things:
from insect to far raptor
intimation flexes, like a bird's eye.

High on the columnar trunk of the day nests the sun.

2.

How loosely twist the unresurrected dead, the stalks and leaves,
they glow like the deathly radiance of the infant
not dead, simply asleep in incandescence,
a kind of marble that grows hourly — marmoreal, metabolic.

Everything is refurbished in its own specific decay.
This then is the harvest in which maturity is universal,
things are felled and they still stand,
the scythe strikes them, they stand immortally ripe in prematurity
and in fact nothing has changed but the light.

3.

And in this clearing, as though a slab had been removed,
the empty casket thus exposed glows not with disappointment
nor with intuitions of any apotheosis —
merely a volume, a crypt even, that, unlidded, provides a space
we now may take with us, build into us, into which we may step
in safety forever after, whatever spies and thieves
think they have wired and traced the chambers of our sweet resort.
This is the coffin that frees us, sarcophagal liberty,
impregnable Egypt, our agile tomb.

Thus may we incubate the empty nest we find, last season's.
So the fragments of last summer's eggshells
assemble in our minds, not reconstructed but scattered,
strewn over the darkened and loosened fibres of an overwintered cup
and they are asylum more than any human shard, all personal history.
What has broken remains so. Diaspora is integrity.

Winter Wren and Spring Rain

Rain and the wren's song
from the ravine of fir and ivy,
the song diffused by the rain
yet rendered in this way
more moistly penetrating
even as the rain is penetrating,

as though moisture had the power
to soak up music and to expand it
in sudden, sodden resonance . . . A paradox
because the wren's song in drought time
cascades, as a cup that runs over.

Can damp then absorb — can it amplify
damp? Like a slug the song travels
and does not travel, glistening robustly
over terrain it resembles.
Or does the song humbly blur
among the shaking raindrops
the way a spill of liquid reaches,
as with a will, with a muscle,
across intervening space
to join and compound with
kindred damp? So the mushroom
towers roundly from clamminess,
itself clammy and distilled at once.

The song moves trammelled
by kinds of wetness
as vines bind in soddenness
the slowed hiker's ankles.

Leaf, water, twig and web:
the hiker's leg cannot tell one
feeling from another. All
convey the impression of greater
impediment than is actually
presented. Yet this brimming is real
and we cup it in confusion,
being drenched and not slaked, thirsting
in the midst of the musical deluge
for this — the same musical deluge.

Rain after Clear

We hated the winter rain
but with its intermission and its resumption
knowledge of its alliance with us
brims a reservoir:
we taste with mollusc adhesiveness
the cold footsole against linoleum,
we sense how the air is more supportive
of our love for indolence and enclosure
and this saturation seems deliberately
to make a show, not quite convincing,
of impassability, discouraging us
exactly according to our wish —

an exhortation to sloth,
to take for our sloppy clock
the vague heavy drip from the drainpipe,
a full splattering accompaniment
to the monosyllabic chirp of the damp sparrow
and the beat, hardly regarded,
of the interminably saturated heart.

And then how passively fat
the first stalks of plants ooze from the loam
dissenting out of a bulkier
laziness from seclusion in earth,
as though growth were a superior disregard,
indolence the slovenly avenue to virtue.

History of Petals

On still days pollen is diffused
and like a greater tree around the tree
there is a hazy invasion, you brim uneasily
with this fertility
as though a wrong hormone were gently injected
and you fell sick with spring.

But comes a grey day, now you sip perfume,
it seems swimming around you silvered
as a swan moves with impervious breast over a pond.
So the whole season is offered you to drink
and this generosity takes you, this excess
of which you accept a just measure.
You swim and you drink, you float and you do not dive.

And a windy day casts down the petals like the glances of elated children
whose blows against each other do not bruise, but exhilarate.

Then build the drifts of still-bright blossoms in the gutter.
If your toes brush through them there is resistance,
a soggy tugging, as when the small wave, having
risen up the beach around you
pulls back at you and the sand under your soles,
a tide followed by the hard yellow of dandelions
that stick behind in the dark fierce grass.

Jupiter the Woodpecker

The leaves have not found their full shape yet,
their incompleteness tickles the trunks' nerveless bulk
of which they are the impossible expression of levity.
The tickling has hardly any effect.
The trunks stand to another edict.
That is the laughter of the woodpecker, laughter
without laughter, a making more vertical
of the vertical trunks, a call to attention
somewhere between fear and mirth.
The beak of the woodpecker probes for rottenness
but its cry imposes integrity on a core.
I cannot see it, the pileated
woodpecker, somewhere it raises its crest,
scrabble its scaly toes, shift
its black and red, its tail as stiff
as something life has discarded
and dry death has lightly taken up.
The Romans made the woodpecker
Jupiter's bird and it builds of the forest
a temple centred on affectless exultation,
altar-side rapture, hilarity of sacrifice.
Like the tallest of trees, Douglas fir, super-eminent
the voice is everywhere audible, a pole of sound
up and down which the beak strikes
for decay, consolidating the slow-grown
temple's open and frightening aspiration
and pleading for the fire of heaven.

Bushtits

> *"A tiny nondescript brownish grey bird of southwestern British Columbia. Lack of any definite markings."* — Birds of Canada

Here they come like a mild obsession —
victors over the inertia of the garden.
Kindly ten or thirty take a tree
by triumphant telepathy, thoughts
assuming without conquering
a mind. Birds, they look like parts
of birds: a third of tail is their whole
tail, a fifth of a body their whole
body. Too small their eyes shine
to impart glitter at our distance
yet covertly their voices brighten,
curving into the ear's view and
sinking, bending as though
deaf to themselves, almost at once
lost: they find, they mimic for our ear
what the eye sees of dark leaves
which illumination barely scrapes.
These birds, these thoughts, come as
candidly as though the tree, the mind
had never known humiliation
or its own hunched, dim mendacity —
neither shame of malady, nor mistakes.

The flock sifts among the arboreal
accumulation, the leaf-whole, the leaf-blasted,
and gently and brokenly coruscates
a moral: it's not oblivion, but setting aside
that redeems our hellish heads,
and forgiveness need not come —
just this grey, slim teeming.

So heaven visits, brown stars,
mousy bits and pieces foraging
among sundry derelictions.

Listen how our foliage of wrong offers nourishment.

Lagoon

Melancholy is as real as arthritis:
the blue heron suffers from both
and for all the depth of its scrutiny
cannot distinguish one from the other.
Around the pond the birches drop
their uncastable colour, heavenly
yellow brings sky down with it, infusing
saturated loam with celestial, crumbling
levity. The heron is a piece of landscape
slower than the windy remainder of world,
more stalled even than the irremovable
mantle of duckweed. Infinitesimal birds,
chickadees, sparrows, are like
abortive resolutions of the heron,
quick as caffeine but too weak
to lift scaly feet planted in the clay
of sadness, stuck in wet reflection
as though a mirror were an anchor,
the pond a burden, unliftable,
the clouds a worse burden, the blue neck
twisted in a tortuous crick,
every joint clotted, as though
with the whole forest's wet leaves
burdened — unsustainable, stained garland
on the brow of a conscious statue, which hurts.

The Broken Eggs of the World

Sleep Sink

As though waking were air and sleep water
the girl passes from one to the other in the arms of her mother.
As her mother lowers her into the crib and, she sinking,
the girl gleams and shines as through nightfall air, nightfall water,
I bend my knees and kneel to lapse with her
crouching now at the level where mattress whitens
against crib's darkly gleaming bars. She extends a hand
between the bars, moistened from her mouth two fingers,
and she slaps me lightly for a confirmation, she smiles, she retracts,
she curls up and she smiles with lips curled around two fingers,
index, middle, she has sucked herself into herself
like a moon plunged to the bottom of a lake.

My daughter has sunk like an anchor. I dive after.
She's the anchor I lost with my father when, sky darkening,
we sailed lost on a lake ringed by stone, night ascending
like a swimmer dripping oblivion from his shoulders
and coolness rose, and fear, and awareness of how
all rock is really hard potential of pain. We peered down,
we saw the anchor descending slowly, as calmly
as a broad, notched leaf or a hand
that plays at mimicking fall of a leaf —
into the dark and darker tilting, uniting
with dissolution of depth. We dove after it, colder,
light in water beyond extinct, the water denser,
a shudder developing from within us
as we dissolved in dissipating heat, dissipating hope.

It was lost. It anchored itself in the bed, the bedrock of night
and look, father dead, I found it here, gripping, anchored,
keeping all the dreams down that she will forget, my daughter.

Sunday Afternoon

1.

By temperament you savoured gradation,
yet all was black and white in your office and it taught me
(the linoleum, the desks, the outmoded appliances
bequeathed unmodified from the past of the city)
that, though there labours dumbly a principle of mass production,
there is no such thing, no such thing as mass
consumption. Those quizzical objects could not
be assimilated to any imaginable use unless
it be the raw material of reverie.

And, even when they were used, those things —
as illegible to me as hieroglyphs — evinced
a surplus that escaped into something else, totemic,
incurable by the sensible rejoinders to my questions,
on those Sunday afternoons bottomed by linoleum
squares black and white, coiled about by your
cigarettes' self-diffusion, self-immolation
so that always I rubbed my eyes in mixed
wonder and irritability, denizen of an ashtray's
bottom — yet happy, there, as those young Vikings
(the scholars tell us), those young men
called by the name of *cinder biters*. They lolled
among the cold hearth-leavings lethargically
exempt from a role — worker, warrior — in the longhouse:
or their purpose was to be ashen, as light
as ashes in the palm, as heavy as ashes
when their fume confuses the chest, pervading
the inner and outer worlds alike, the body's office
of breathing and the law office itself, its chambers.

2.

Even now, I can't invent a plausible use
for that box-like rough-surfaced grey machine.
It ticked its mensuration in your office corner.
I look through your door and I see
the bamboo-patterned drapes, as yellow
as nicotine, drawn against the more yellow sun
where a cigarette became an ongoing cremation
managed so quickly and so deftly. Those Sunday
afternoons formed a still oxbow in the city's
river. Or we waited, we children, like the inmates
of an Egyptian tomb, immortally withering
as millennia passed. No one knocked in the slab
with a hammer, or fell into the flaw in the roof.

The sign on your door said SOLICITOR: not
enough. I don't know what your own office in life
actually was — solicitor of flame, of smoke, of black
and of white, a stillness of thought even greater
than that issued by the slow flame, slow smoke,
the ticking of that imponderable metre. Was it
the ticking of Justice? The mills of the gods?
It was Sunday downtown — a sense of tolerable suffocation,
diversion with adult stationery passing the childish hours,
the world stationary, the clock stationary, the aged
freight elevator stationary and then came supper
at last, at home, where your pained wife moved
resentfully in a joyous aroma of fat and time. Time,
like a breaker released from a retrograde
current, curled toward Monday, toward school
flushing the ashes away like a spring tide.

Colborne Street

I was the gargoyle of your stone office in the off hours,
hours achieving neither silver nor violet in the sky
but gaining the coloration of weariness, decency
and flirtatious attrition mixed. And in those hours I hunched
and out of them I thrust my neck for dark provender,
like a night heron roosted, worshipful, opposing
the verdigris spike of the cathedral, green after
green falling prey to falling night. We never once
attended it where it tapered beyond the fly-specked
blank and glitter of the parking-lot — cars shrunk
as bugs upended, crashed in your sandstone
window-corner, the near fire escapes lowered
diffidently as onto a crooked planet so long derelict
all was novelty again among the dumpsters
dented like meteorites, the ailanthus
cracking fume-cramped air with its branches and splitting
the sidewalk with its roots and broken
bracchiation of its shadows, the gulls
hustling with their beaks of knives forever drawn
and the pipes kinked as desire so obstinate
it cannot flex into opportunity, but only
add another crimp to impacted convolution while
a hiss issues from valves shaped like fruition
calloused into mineral . . .

And newly inflecting the gravel, tar, mortar, plastic,
shaking shreds of billboards and filaments
in dead bulbs and thrumming cinereous glass
against which, somehow, the seraphic shit of ringbills
had splashed up and a spider stretched ethereal
trickery engrossed now by coarse caddis-fly
casing of demolitional grit, and past
the huddled pigeons matted like lint

from the laundromat, mangy as motel pillows
threadbare with balding dreams and among handbags
reamed out by thieves, cyclopean city hall
clock clanged, and all was vibrant
whether broke or lucky, cracked, sodden
or racked by coughs within the outward-moving
circuit of those bells plowing the discoloured
dusk like the rusted bows of a lake freighter
and just as in the strong, corroded
collar-grab of this clamour

I am sustained still in your embrace, vibration
fathoming shadow-bottoms, dust flung up to a gong,
steely rubigo ennobled by sunset and all urban bruises by blue night,
sweep of tarnished wings oratorical then subtle
from a rough-faced tower making me shake
with the tolling of love and rattling the flaking frame
of love and stretching out my love, gargoyle-faced,
ratty, heron-gawky, for the life you have given me
this long that even now warps around the twists
of that skyline like a nighthawk collecting (intent
on its distraction) a rare, raw diet of downtown
diptera, skirting the satellite dishes hollow and deaf
to the toxic fecundity of their locale,
cocked like prayers for rays of remote blessing —

how they ignore the kingly dilapidation from which, so strenuously
empty, they crane to catch what already holds them fast

as a bell its sonorousness, as rust its seized valve.

The Tongue

For its shape we named the peninsula but
the only voice, often, was the remote
whitethroat's and, nearer, the hiss of waxwings
which matched the slenderness of grasses
and conifer spindles. Insects made noise but not
with their mouths. The tongues belonged to birds
and the birds had fibrous tongues, not pulpy
like ours, tongues like thorns, lips as hard
as nails. Acute rock-flanks were slick
with loose caps of moss and shallow fern.

Hemlock shadow makes immediate night.
The moths swarmed like stars called
to stage their constellations abruptly.
Those trees exude almost no scent, no balsam fragrance,
and when we climbed among the branches,
they held the suffocated atmosphere
of a closet not opened for a long time,
where we shouldn't have been, and where
clothes of an epoch before our birth
had hung. My father's buffalo robe,
my mother's dancing gear, youth turned
into a dryly rotting museum in this closet
long time made. We felt the content
that comes of knowing that even the extinct
is perpetuated, and what has not yet come to be
comes to pass now, and nothing
we consider personal doesn't appear
impersonally, not in a closet perhaps
but open like a sky with stars, violated,
inviolate, represented beyond us and within us
as passingly we explore the peninsula
among a few sounds, a few scents
inside hemlock's daylight dark.

The Bluffs

Everything had grown into this array, rock
and bird voice had reached accord.
The world had been tuned like a stringed
instrument, the pine to the towhee,
the towhee to the vein of quartz, the moss
to the bristly caterpillar, and the millipede
in the groin damp beneath the lid of stone
agreed in every principle with the spangled
sunfish radiant sideways where the lily pads
expanded rounded leaves, from which alone
of all plants visible the appearance of dew
never departed.
                    We dangled legs from the rock,
stone as with affection scraped our calves
and the bay was a fish shining in its scales
and the boulders glinted with micaceous scales,
the black-throated green warblers wore
long light cool scales for plumage,
the scales of the cedars were like the scales
loosing spores beneath fern fronds,
the sun glittered like a shed snakeskin
and what of Cain and Abel afflicted our flesh
was purged like the bare bones we found
that winter polished and summer burnished —
little deaths so lively the curled-up bones
recollected coronal ground nests.

Perfection quick in concord hatched from them
under our eyes, in our hands, at our feet
so long as we let the good hour seat us.

The Beaverpond

In that hot, sodden place you could
forget the fate of everyone.

Forget all lands. All losses.
Love, even, you could forget,
envy and hate, religion,
because you had brought
the aluminum canoe to the beaverpond.

The beavers had dammed up peace, no not
peace, they had dammed up this place
flooding away all other places, sinking
history. Oblivion as effective as Noah's
deluge, though no bigger than a field.
While breathing the bright air
you, too, were drowned.

Like a rampart sentinel pacing
the flaming limit of all things,
a red-tailed hawk secured perception's
perimeter, turning an insurpassable circle.
As constantly as a mother on her intact brood
all day it was the broken eggs of the world
that the sun so warmly incubated.

Water-snake-slim, you paddled past nude trees,
you conveyed yourself over the dripping
slippery floor. You sat in an elongated
chair as warm as the day. You inspected a gallery
of totem poles which nest-builders
animated. Here a hooded merganser
glared from its punk cavern, there a tree swallow
twittered like a more brutal butterfly. Even
a venturesome starling, so far from the cities,
so alien to this water carrying the images
of logs like a cool mosaic of disaster
as calm as catastrophe recollected in an afterlife —
even a starling looked out from a cavity.
It had stolen that hole. It was at home.

The Outcrop

Never did you come into that solitude without a master, nothing
you learned alone, there was always a guide. You mounted
from the forest of hemlocks by the stones set almost
like a staircase, where the blazes you made, once, with your brother
had dulled — mildly — flaked off in mild decay — and now the
     summer-parching
swamp lamp-lit by redstarts, with its whining gyres
of itchy mosquitoes, its blackflies like influxes
of bothering thought, constantly trying the strength
of any one steady mood, all of it dropped behind . . .

Red oaks on the domed rocks want of nutriment had stunted.
Yet they had the beauty of having been restrained, like knowledge
which only comes late or — if it comes early — is forgotten
and later with effort retrieved, a stone so heavy
fingers can only half manage to turn it over. Pads of moss
the drought had made bristly and the intimate fume
of rock tripe, like old clothes, like evaporated love,
blew across the varied rock as a memory
on which you seek to found your support, not a gravestone
nor yet a cenotaph, a memorial for your pleasures
that recurs to you — a perfume the poorly remembering
wind sometimes recalls to you, on its oblivious wanderings
oblivious of this, too: oblivious of the service it renders you.
Stone had balanced on stone since the rule of the glaciers,
only bears' paws had modified this erratic sculpture,
seeking white grubs from weight's underside and time's.
Stumps rotted like shipwreck remains in a polder.

Far off the blue of the bay was hard and separate
from the hot rock, its heat not a mammal's but a reptile's ,
as distinct as the hull of a canoe from the water,

someone else steers in the stern. You wield your paddle
at what seems your will, though there is a guide even in your solitude.

First and Last Things

Night Park

As cyclonic swifts focus their horde
on the exiguous chimney of their night roost,
vacillating satellites hostage to
the psychomachia of sun and moon,
and oblivion sucks down just one at a time,
and the rest are defiant, as though to suspend sleep
signified a moral victory and the sustained
temptation to fall were already identical with
the triumph of virtue (temptation being the most
inexhaustible engine, a perpetuum mobile
planing the skyline like a circular saw),
and fatigue's casualties flake from the vortical
orbit, excommunicated from the circuitous cult
of the visible like the chlorotic rays of the sun —

so around the clipped dictates of the boxwood hedges
and around the superbly standing wave of the housefronts,
around the phragmites shivering by the pond
like nakedness excited or cold nakedness for sale,
around the loosestrife lanterns and the gilt
adornment flaking from black water,
around the mallard ducks' fear — concentrics
flexing out from plump hulls of misgiving —
and around the hortensia browning in its urn
(blighted petals like the bruises of the rest),
and around the intenser nights long since roosting
in clenched trees that keep their eclipse like jealous gods,
ignorant Lust goes spinning nightly,

a rowboat that pivots on a single oar,
pressed always forward by limbo's brood of options
(launch, they cry, launch the formation of the future's body) —
but Lust finds children quite inconceivable
though it may pace nightly around the wrought-iron playground staves
and around the cement coast of the circular wading pool
and the simple carousel propelled by hand —

Lust cannot learn, it only swerves;
eyes flash tossing on its cruising rim,
it twists on the heel of its vicious circle,
it banks blackly as a swift deferring the narrow way to sleep;

and when it succumbs, it will have burst into tomorrow
and from a tall roost the dawn wanderers will disperse
having gestated the night,

leaving not in circles but in tangents
of some more wayward and more genial manifestation of desire.

Cara

You were drunk. So was I. Yet lightly drunk
as cabbage butterflies around the wild carrot
in their vintage clothing vortical, becomingly.
On your glass heels you tottered. "Tottering" isn't
the right word, you were levitating as though
in surprise this gift came to you. Taperingly
you seemed in danger of falling, in the safer
folly of lifting. We were runny and glassy
with circling wine, white wine, and behind
plate glass the café goers saw us in green
dusk light as those in a zoo realize at once
there is no enclosure. Glass is all the membrane
between our joy and their exclusion, their
voyeur's consolation, as between the diver, the fish.

Gently the green light flooded us. Our
bodies swam in that wide lapping lightness
of June twilight and of wine, your kisses
washed over me warmly as when your kisses
half in the caressing surf, surrendered to an ocean
blood warm, spit warm, and white wine
charity is a tidal pool of the same uterine
threshold. Sea's long kiss of coast, twilight
the lovemaking of day and night, and the city itself
is love, parental, filial, fraternal, amorous
of strangers for strangers, for who, building
the oppression of that stacked, cracked factory,
could imagine the sequential charities of its
kindled sumac- and fox-coloured bricks?

Our pollutions are purifications. Nothing, Cara,
can be soiled. Violation is not possible, my love,
though it feels real. It feels real. As gulls
against a white wall, as crows in dusk silhouette,
we were lost, foundering in concolour congruity,
pleonasms of good fortune, 1983.

Deliverance

With thunderbolt and mild melt
winter, terrible parent, perishes,
who frosted our hands into fists
commanding us make
what figures of revolt
our repetitive bodies permit us,
secluding us also sourly in cloth.

Finally granted, freshly fork the roads.
Craning for the lane that leads all lanes

O children, O bereaved, where turn we now?

Fingers, limbs by the mighty
isometric of bearing up under much
have swollen and, fierce, crush the gifts.

Yes we do, we want
as twigs to be spirited to that dove's nest,
woven to be and well bent
and jobless again but for rage of bondage

with our wrathful malleable fellows
strong in the measure in which we are stuck.

Holotype
"Specimen on which the description of a new species is based"

1735. June morning. I stepped out with legs
inexhaustibly strong, not being
called upon to exhaust themselves. And my
chin tilted upward like a frog's to tongue a fly,
I averred as recklessly as a lover's vow
*Twittering tongue and wing, that bird's not a
swift but The Swift* and, though the bird couldn't hear,
I emphasized the point, repeating
the name twice *The Swift The Swift*
in syncopation as close as the wingbeats of the bird or
as the headiness of the whole flock fired,
torrid with birds' blood, from the month's
green cannonmouth. *The Swift The Swift* said I
Otherwise in Latin — a tongue I'm proud to know —
Apus apus. And the name stuck though other
particulars of that day have fled the brain,
as fugitive as the swifts' own sweep and hissing
mentation scoured out of south
Sweden's slender, unimpressionable ether.

And so every swift on every morning subsequent,
no matter the hour, flew instantly
a latecomer and every swift you ever saw
twitched, however swift, laggardly in the wake of my chosen one
who abraded, who buffed the Swedish sky — weather's
volatile soul of an ice age, its
igneous-metamorphic outcrops of climate, those
bouldery ghosts of glaciers, clouds,
so much weight held in laughing
suspension. Don't deride my original
euphoria as possessive . . .

Stop pointing the finger. I never
secured all swifts, the baptism was

exact — a modest manner of augury. Holotypical
is the world forever, every specimen
of everything is representative, and day (the first
day) breaks
daily like June 1735. Must I, Carolus
Linnaeus, perform forever, in the display
case of resentment, the holotype of your cowardice?
Perpetuate *Scapegoat*, hardy genus?

Did I not demonstrate, with, admit,
more than common finesse, the classic touch —
the new, singular, simple, successful shock
we crave with every intake of our scornfully
trite lives?

                Primary instance!
To live by grace of all swift examples!
To meet lucent wind as an equal with the breast
of the first of the flock upward toward which
height of land respires polar balm
of early principles, meadow sighs out
first fruits while all around the clouds, uncommitted
to a configuration, break their mould
without blood loss or forfeiture of honour,
as frivolous and serious as Ovid?

This is The Swift said I. *In the beginning is
this Swift.* I was with it, and it was with the
beginning, and sibilantly The Swift
took me there, crepitant, on crescent wings.

For we know nothing but first and last things.

Hortus Botanicus

1.

Here from germination, from the act of sowing,
names attend the growths they designate.
Each has a label in legible script.
Our hosts, the blossoms, are less ephemeral
than we who crunch the pebble path and admit
flowers to the nose and eye in a single
inhalation. The loveliest name, we decide,
is *Anemone nemorosa*, Greek and Latin,
deep forest's breezy flower. Linnaeus
said it bloomed only on the first day
the Swedish swallow's returning wing shook
the bud's uncompacting petals. But —
given the profusion here — for a novice
to adjudicate just to which plant the name
belongs is hard to determine with certainty.
The advent of a swallow would help, perhaps.
Yet here there are only coots and ducks
raving in canals dotted with sopping bread.

2.

Look how belladonna dilates the Jacobean
black and intrigue of its berries: a greenhouse
is a place where forced desire becomes
desire. And that potted palm, there, has subsisted
exactly the same, as formal as carved rays
complicating the haloes of an altar-piece
while three hundred years passed its window
glass, bearing swords and bouquets in their grasp.

3.

Today I am not resentful, not one to cry
*Away with these names, would that I could come
here before names, before Eden, Adam,
the act of naming.* The names I've learned, fixing
them poorly in the tissue of my brain — like moths
that the pin missed, and they flutter freely
so I have to make of my mind a flame of sorts
strong enough to attract, weak enough
not to scorch them — the names I've learned
I got with some pleasure in discipleship. I
am glad of Linnaean binomials, trinomials,
glad of human arbitrariness, art
making nature more natural. *Genus* and *species*
balance economy and elaboration,
resembling in structure the low flight over
the canal of that bridge, embellished selectively
in a way that doesn't consolidate
its sturdiness, but makes the transition more
decoratively conscious. Abstract words
make the eye see more concretely as we pace,
delighted by the vibrations, over
that reverberant arch of painted planks.

4.

Like children, the ignorant latest generation,
we mount worn, very high, very
wide marble steps, we grasp these names
and haul our gauche mortality along.
Linnaeus is antique; his insights have rotted.
But was eternity ever the question for us?
And just as a baby points wordlessly,
and the parent answers *That's a lily,
and that's a rose,* and the child shows she's
satisfied by agreeing to move on, unstuck
from the snag of curiosity which springs
as recurrently as a footstep,
so for us the names improve our vision
by augmenting the array of what we perceive.
Our minds grip a balustrade our ancestors
carved with more care than vanity,
with here a Silenus and there a Ceres,
a Juno, a Triton, a Venus, good company,
and awkwardly and felicitously we pass
all the shrines of this formally grown pantheon
as the flower-fugitive guests of the season.

Gorgias the Magician

Oh yes, Gorgias the magician did finally make it
to our town. He came to our glass tavern, the glass
dirty, cracked, strung with spiderwebs, flyspotted —
the genius condescended to grace our glass tavern.
We knew him from his portraits, you know
he has them painted every three years. We knew
that too-trim black beard, that furry condensation
of illimitable self-care, we knew that black close
hair, the dilating pale bald spot and the black-
pupilled eyes vainly magisterial but scattered
at the touch of someone's stronger will
like a pond shocked at insolence of a sided pebble.
He meant his famous picture to say: Invincible mask.

He has his portrait, the one retouched exactly every
three years, paraded even through dumps like ours
by strong acolytes, boys, all of them, and all too stupid
to understand even the easiest of his spells. Those boys
trudge the dangerous paths because they march
under his breakable spell (a special execration
against the will of women meant to break
the will of men), and off they trot, the boys,
to carry his picture in a tasselled litter passengered
also by a gaudy statuette of our Blessed Virgin.
It's the just way the Romans lugged ancestral busts
in a chaise during a funeral procession, swaying.

But now Gorgias was actually here in the flesh, he
grasped our disjointed podium and spoke
into our crackly microphone, avoiding the thick worn cord.
He did look like his painting — but his hands shook, hard,

they shook even when we shook them, though they
looked strong if only you could still them, vibrating
like the abdomens of incited wasps, incited injured wasps.
And when he read from his falsely antiquated scrolls
embarrassed pity made us fidget — for he meant so clearly,
we being boys, he meant clearly
to catch us in the oracular cages of his syntax,
but the sophistry of the work was such that the bars
stood as far apart as lamps posted to dispel the night
on a trivial avenue. The shadow of his hand
on the wall shook to make the semblance of
the crown of a tossing tree so that even, you thought,
the roots shook loose, and we pretended to go into
Gorgias's bad old cages, we feigned our capture, we applauded
his magic with shaking hands as though debility were ours,
delusion ours, and we escorted him in the insult
of our kindness to the hinge-loose glass door. Beyond
it, our well-founded trees as firm as rock
found a pleasure in the night breeze they pleasured
with a sound that tickled like the love of heaven . . .

But by then our malice had already infected
the heartwood of our sweet trunks, for contempt
kills centre and periphery, withers the heart
and dries the pulse in the wrist sapped of charity.

Styx

The ferryman before he left the deck said
Enough to scare the shit out of you, isn't it?
He meant the horn, the boat's sobbing horn
blown to warn of the advent of the vehicle.
He left then. He had stolen shore leave.
And I had been appointed for the duration
the pilot of the stream, the channel that fog always
shrouds, the fog that souls express, the fog of souls
standing shoulder to shoulder and breathing
their dead breath into each others' luminous
opacity to suspend, indispellably,
a bank of ground-level cloud hugging
the river's bled circuitousness. Despite
the legends you hear, none of the souls ever
gets across Acheron. The ferry unloads
its mortal freight into the air above the stream
where fog, which is hell, thickens forever. On both
banks of Acheron earthly life blithely dwells
and the river remains as good as invisible
under hell's occluding vapour, the colour of cataracts
filming a senile eye. Blank leisure is all
excepting the horn's tusk and beam and wake . . .

That suspirious instrument, I suppose, warns other
shipping on the stream. But what traffic could share
the channel with the dead, with the ferry? Fog (did you
know), fog, which is death, echoes? Yields back
longer cry than the blast of the horn that lent it voice.
I've never heard a response to the horn or
to its echo. On the deck I noticed how my own
shadow, cast by the boat's beacon onto a wall
of fog, stood there like a soul stained indelibly.

The fluent water worried greyly like rock
troubled by a dream of fossils, labile
trilobites, elusive ferns and instantaneous
dragonflies. What was the point of a pilot
anyway? Still, my sense of perception seemed
miraculously to sharpen. And why? Because
I realized I had responsibility for the resolution
of things, I tugged the blurred world into focus
with an effort like a horse drawing a barge
down a canal. Cold death-sweat condensed
on my forehead, against posthumous opposition.
Only my life, an error, in its conjuring heron-fixity
hauled the shore closer and caused
the ghostly harvest of bubbles at the bow
that acclaimed our progress, which seemed a stasis.

But where had the ferryman gone? What was he doing?
The few whitecaps embodied a messenger,
the one from Marathon trying — trying again —
the news bursting in a foam tossed on the wave-top,
turf on the swell of a tumulus that crawled away.
The grave now had no victory: neither did my life.
I shuddered, and it seemed my goosebumps raced
in froth across the channel and revolved above the current
through which a dark bird, a murre, emerged and sank
like a birth in a dream, delivered and undelivered.

Then the murre was borne upward in deflectless flight
making fog lucidity — and death, more vivid life.

No Memory of Pleasure Imprisons

1.

Someone envious said: you're in jail. And I asked:
can song — can a singer
imprison? No. For every time
the voice of the singer
merges with memory's voice
that time is now, is now and wide open
moistly like the mouth that first sang, that
sings still. Dawn has opened
wide where the wrens and sparrows
call, mottling broad silence
with the spare intensity of morning
errands and the dew on rose leaves
the day already sips
with the slight-limbed focus of an insect.

Everywhere, on every leaf,
candour of water is the only maculation;
there is attrition only of cleanliness
as the gentle towel kisses away
the bather's moisture —

I hear her voice again, and again her
voice is in me and it is I who
bear her within me, as I
change she changes, yet all seems
unaltered, as season by season
the self-identical birds
mutate from and toward
exactly what this most exacting
globe dictates — no prison, no
prison but

wingbeats ever and again responsive
to the dire fashions of heaven
adjusted constantly by the beautiful God . . .

2.

Then Charles Darwin was no singer
of strict necessity, his theme was
to necessity there is
an over-plus, even beyond sexual beauty . . .
Or sexuality beyond mating, procreation,
beyond even
creation, beautiful
necessity. Beyond
creation there lies another
beauty. Memory carries her voice
inside me, our voices walk
together arm in arm, the gravel
whitely crepitates this
morning as we age
and do not age, two birds
in remembrance of song, which is
song also. Song is what holds
the marrow-less thin-muscled
wing stretched above oceans and cities.

Listen to the wind. Some things
harmoniously impede it now
as wit, some now as penitence,
some now as neither. And what is
that? No prison, it is song.

Wrong

Wrong. We're wrong — all wrong — but right, all
right in this weather whose edict cuts
strictly, easily, hazy alighting of pleasure
in precincts of hard-edged desolation,
and so, somehow, some wrongs we commit
evade wrongdoing
as haze avoids shape's
finality. Is that broad

blurred beam — almost
warm, as though we ourselves had to warm it
and became all the warmer for passing on our warmth —
is that ray really the efflux of an infernal sun?
The sun is, after all, a fiery bomb in space
continuously bombing itself.
Though not today. No. The description
just doesn't match. We must keep warm the sun —
so poor, so generous. It wants to be warm; it is very nearly warm.
With our help (which is wrong), the sun will grow warm.

Now the day perches like a bird on a finger,
the day as mild as the breast feathers of a bird.
Yet not just one hard beak but the almost
insupportable rigours of the real sky,
which never simply agrees to lift anything,
preened that plumage
into a fabric of supernal gentleness.

While we can, let's lift on our own palms
this soft hour, like a bird — the hour's unfocused,
dilated sun. And like a clearing in the forest
is the wrong we commit: no wrong at all,
but a place where pursued things pause,
relaxed even though every particular of their form
answers and keeps answering — as it must —
to the wrong righteousness that fires the universe.

Hunted

Being hunted is surprisingly easy.
You would think you would lose
your concentration on what you want
to think about. Not so. Or that
the sound of the wind in the high fir tops
would come to signify only
fear. No. That wind blows straight
to wherever the pleasure in wind
reaches, the sound of hardship
and of solitude when neither
is pressing — evocation
rather than experience. Evocation
overcomes experience. Experience
is less experience, sometimes,
than the notion of another life —
one you've never had, or did have
so long ago you were someone else. Birds
likewise. They fly in and among
the pains of persecution
and dispel those pains. What
pains? And gradually it doesn't
matter to you that you are hunted
and known in the main by the hunter's
wrong emphases. How well the hunter
scrutinizes field-marks, but field-marks
have nothing to do with evocation:
the scars of experience, they're simply
those. Perhaps if the hunter aims
at experience and its field-marks
he will miss, and you — you may
escape, being a creature of evocation
and thus not subject to the hunt.

Thaw
Sullivan's Pond, Dartmouth

Each morning pebble melted out of snow
bears on its back, like a knapsack of self-confidence,
the precise blue supplement of its shadow
as clear as the craters of the moon —
a face diagrammed in recollection
with economy not precluding love.
Ice deep under its shield weeps away stoicism;
hoarse ducks revolve within the dilating
edges of the pond's diaphragm of slush
as if their quack rubbed them wider passage
and they were midwives to the hedonism of water's sass.
So the whistling of chickadees and starlings
diffuses invention, not that the compositions are new
but rather that the routes they have found
stream past the season's sag and shatter
like melting icicles, elliptical reiterations
to syncopate the longueurs of paralytic air.
Between crisp and lax, grass equivocates
into the air more richly, creamy with reflux
of warmth that makes each exhalation an act
of manumission. It mollifies embittered
wind so cold it lost its sense of smell
rigidly ruffling drifts' sunken carcass fringes,
frayed flags of car dealerships and twisted
ringbill pinions jutting from stopped eddies.

And understated esperance, like a song
sparrow almost out of hearing,
is what each next breath and step punctually fulfill
and tease to the rhythm of new-suspended hope
as gulls, grey-brown blowzy hens,

extend across the air their spattered frame of grace
mistakable for purpose. Like a puddle
polishing thinning ice, the result is clear
though the logic of the cause remains as vague as melting
and threatens to shiver into smiles.

Infancy's Visionary Tactility

A Baby's Bent Head

Pensive as a boulder, the volume of thought
perfectly flush with the dome of its idea,
flossy over the scalp with light growing
indistinguishably from hair —
hair and light one indisseverable filament —
moss of infant incandescence across mild rock,
preposterous maturity as though a bud
might rightly succeed a blown flower,
concentration as relaxation, bone
and flesh sibling in softness and the brow
profound, frownlessly, in its meditation,
this head, drooping, exerts a pull on our esteem
as though to bend the world's precocious petals
around its compression, obliging
obeisance to its simple inclination,
a half-nod bottomless like a god's
though wet, perennially, with snail dawdle
of drool which haltingly drips and
stickily like a primordial water clock
whose stalactite ought to, but doesn't form.

Rock, Ball

This hero two years old onto a peninsula wobbles.
The embracing birches, beeches and oaks are to him
impassable and their crisscross roots dislodging
or enwrapping bits of stone form an impediment,
the nurse of reverie, pitting lingering eye against
the elastic, exploratory foot. The foot
loses. Reverie pronounces three determinations: *Tree* . . .
Rock . . . *Moss*. The limit, almost, of the child's
lexicon, given the milieu. He slaps the tree trunks
with both palms, slaps rock, pokes moss
as though it were the yielding of his own belly,
or part of himself with which his diaper
keeps him hours a stranger. Hitting
one boulder, bulging congruously from the shore,
flecked with biotite mica and with lichens,
he pronounces *Rock Rock Rock* as though
his interlocutor were the deferential little waves
raising blunt reflexes of sun for him — mirrors, minor
magi. *Rock Rock* he says to the gross stone
then *Ball Ball*. Smoothness the warted
boulder lacks, it lacks buoyancy, it isn't especially
spherical yet the propriety of ball remains
allowable, even to the eavesdropper. *Ball* the boy
claims. The boulder leaps, invisibly
recoiling, into another class of things. As if to a dog
the boy had blurted *Bird*, with a tongue that pats
like a child's palm, too hard. No dog could shake off
the label. A boulder lodged ten thousand years
rolls on a clean two-year-old tongue, rolls wide of it
and bounces, leaving immobile an abandoned
twin sunk among head-hanging sedge in its attitudes

of neoclassical graveyard woe, yes sunk
like a foundation on which everyone depends
and which everyone forgets, the cornerstone
this sanguine builder seems minded to discard,
stumbling as though stumbling were dexterity.

Reading

Never forget this, the two children leaning
over the book from either side, pressure,
warmth of their bodies, as though they compressed
their mass of life to the utmost mammal
essence, while their almost querulous effort
to understand the planets alternates
with the complacency they have in uttering
what they now, temporarily, know:

what kinds of body are these — are they
celestial? What kind of voice, so
aerial-earthbound, so comforting
as they take comfort, so unaware
of warmth in their warmth, of pressure
in their fine, wide pressure? The book
between us, bright pages open,
pictures taking our eyes in as gravity
pulls a probe through an alien atmosphere,
the round ringed planets with their cores,
their gases, their volcanoes exposed.

The planets burn and freeze and twist around
the more than lethal sun, their seas are frozen
methane, jets of poison spurt their acid arcs
while the firm-soft bodies, the questions
and answers press against the reader.
How fat and interested the listeners are
in all outer space, all craters and fires,
the steady catastrophe of the universe
tamed by the rise and fall of curiosity —

call and response, that grave and childish rainbow,
inflection, covenant the planets cannot know.

September in Uplands Park

What was that odour? Perhaps to call it an "odour"
is already to give it an adequate name, no more
precise name is necessary and none could
dispel the savoury precision of its
saturating vagueness. It wrapped the children
more brightly in their more vibrant clothes,
they ran on the resilient mud and stones
that seemed softened between rows
of snowberries that swelled pellets
of inexact though piercing white. Was it rosehips
that steeped the sky? Or kneeling on moss,
after the first rain for weeks? Or soaking grass that,
for all the fall of water, could not expel
grey-brown from scorched lengths? Was it relief
of ancient rock that the youth of water
stroked it? Was it the oaks, stiff
vehemence doused
with spontaneity, as an accipiter made comic
by being caught in a downpour, glaring
tuft-crazy like someone startled in bed?

All smelled good, and this smell affected
the pace, the gaze, and even the late sun
raised the inexhaustible grey of a cloud to its nose.
To the query came no answer but inhalation, for no
answer right or wrong
resolves a question. Breathing
in, breathing
out mimes the structure
of question and answer.
And is neither.

Wading Willows Beach

Into the water the boy walks. The water seems to brim
alive in a skin and luminous as the boy fills out
his own form, the soft top of his foot and the humped sea-washed
shapes of his toes. The tide is not high or low but swaying
as banners of the seaweed stream in the clarity,
wavery leaf touching the inner water lip as a tongue
in the outswollen skin of the cheek and the other end
trailing and catching to the bottom where, like a crusty
foetus, hard in the deep womb of the world, a crab
diagonals across the sand ribbed as though
in compliance with the sensation the toes transmit
in their syrupy-vitreous magnified tread.

Fish move around the boy as though nudged by the nosy
vibrance of his dimpling thought, showing how our desires
pass on, but not to the point of total estrangement —
he's no junior Tantalus, the desires are not
so elementary that they cannot be postponed and,
besides, the fish behave only as an externalization,
considerate and appealing, of the motive power
we regard as our own, gently decisive though it is
never catching up with itself let alone with its object.

Swaying, finned with tickling, but then so smooth,
the tide is high and wading out of water is needful for a small boy
and all around his fat feet the shore sandgrains batten
attracted by some wish that did not invite these prickling
objects but hoped for some others. We are magnets
that never guess what filings we catch, brushing off our adherents
in complacent conviction, a remedial satisfaction
for the longing we never quite got into focus or lost, either:

so we gain some approximation of our dreams
chafing our feet in the saline breeze that scuffs
soft — soft and gritty — from the weathered blue of the sky.

Primaries

Above jabs of blackflies a May
crow flew over, right wing
short four primaries, parental
silhouette between intact
tree crowns. It flew well, as though
symmetry were superfluous. Do we
ever know the contour of necessity?
The baby was feeling leaves. The crow flew.

Under clouds of jaws and needles we cower
and, besides, we all moult; but some remedy
fills this diverse depletion, as curiosity
animates the jointed flaws of our fingers
making them confederate, consanguineous
with the heady salad of the forest spring
whose compromise begins under the growing
hordes of humming hungers and the hands
of a baby — hands that reject their contours
again and yet again, gaining, fumbling
on the growth of the future, which flies what
it can, as it must, stripped of symmetry,
yet never failing to suggest it.

Pointer
(Girl, 11 months)

She's in the indicative stage, forefinger
extended to show something, and though she knows
little she is my guide and conductor
in the leaf- and painting-hung
world, her moist voice somehow
aerial, like a bird's, and her body
glowing smoothly in each milieu as against
vast intimacy of a fibrous
ensconcement, like an egg in a bird's
nest you have climbed a great height
to discover. And now you, too, repose
in the nest at the end of scaling
to the rim of the beginning of life, here
where the egg rests like a world
roundly to indicate the encompassing
world and from far off a moist-voiced song
tumbles like the blowing of clouds
from the lips of the wind that is always
pointing to where it goes and it never
gets there, but even so it sustains us as it bubbles
along our hearts, ruddying
to the tips of our gestures
the curious sky-fed blood we share.

Acknowledgements

I gratefully acknowledge *Canadian Literature*, *The Dalhousie Review*, *The Fiddlehead*, *The Idler*, *Landmarks*, *The Malahat Review*, *New Canadian Poetry*, and *Ploughshares* for publishing some of this work.

I wish to thank Monique Dull, Iain Higgins, Luke Carson, Ross Leckie, and the Canada Council for the Arts.